I0106593

PRACTICE
THE PAUSE

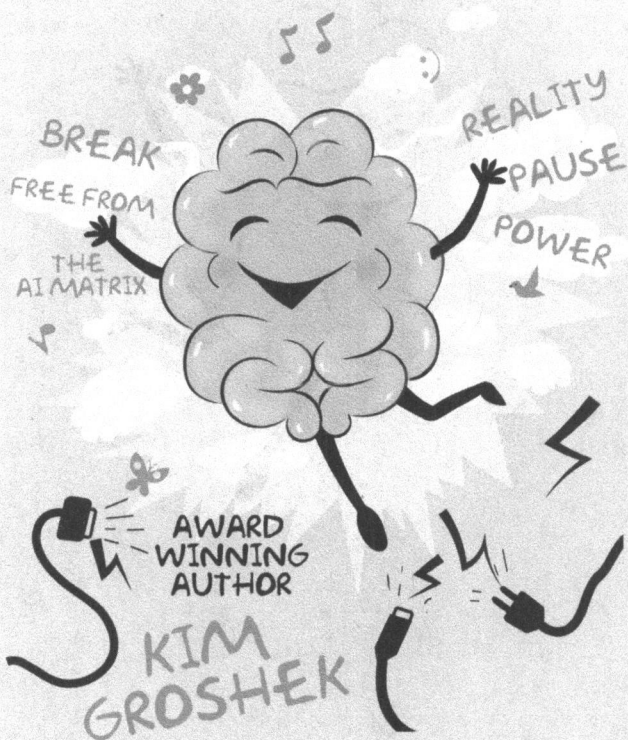

BREAK FREE FROM THE AI MATRIX

REALITY PAUSE POWER

AWARD WINNING AUTHOR

KIM GROSHEK

I want to introduce you to our "Brainy," who will take us into the stories of their head and share what happens when you Uncover your deepest aspirations. Brainy connects with our highest self and becomes all that we indeed are.

PRACTICE
THE PAUSE©

By

KIM GROSHEK

Printed in the U.S.A.

Copyright © 2023 by Kim Groshek

All rights reserved.

ISBN-13: 978-1-942604-03-7

Dedication

I offer my deepest gratitude to my daughter, my partner, and all who have supported me on this journey. You have given me the strength to share my story and the belief that it can make a positive difference in the lives of others. Without you, this book would not exist.

Contents

1

Let's Get Started

Introduction

In a world where artificial intelligence and technology reign supreme, I was entangled in a web of notifications, alerts, and constant connectivity; however, little did I know that this digital paradise would soon become a prison of my own making. As a computer scientist, embracing the digital landscape that promised efficiency and convenience seemed natural.

One fateful day, amidst the cacophony of beeps and buzzes, I realized I had become a slave to the same tools I had created. My senses had dulled, my attention fragmented, and my connection to the present moment severed. In this moment of realization, I decided to embark on a journey of self-discovery, to break free from the AI matrix that held me captive.

With determination, I made a bold decision: to Practice the Pause! I turned off notifications, silenced the constant chatter, and fully immersed myself in the present moment. As the noise subsided, I rediscovered the beauty of stillness and the power of my senses.

As I ventured into the world without the distractions of technology, my senses awakened. I felt fully present for the first time in a long time as the world became more prosperous and colorful. I marveled at the vibrant colors of nature, relished in the symphony of sounds around me, and savored the taste of each meal as if it were a divine delicacy.

With each passing day, my perception of reality shifted. The physical and virtual lines blurred, and I discovered that fact was accessible to screens and algorithms. I began to question the boundaries of what could challenge the limitations imposed by society and technology.

Armed with a newfound sense of empowerment, I sought to break free from the AI matrix that had ensnared humanity. We explored alternative paths, embracing simplicity, mindfulness, and human connection. I connected with like-minded individuals who shared my vision, forming a community dedicated to reclaiming control over our lives.

As I delved deeper into my journey, I realized that the pause away from technology was not just a momentary respite from the expected demands but a gateway to infinite possibilities. With my senses honed and my mind clear, I unlocked hidden talents, pursued new passions, and created a life that was indeed my own.

Through my story, I aim to inspire others to embrace the practice of pausing, awaken their senses, and embark on a transformative journey toward personal empowerment and infinite possibilities. In a world dominated by artificial intelligence, it is essential that we regain control over our lives, redefine our reality, and remember the power that lies within us.

Ultimately, the true revolution is not rejecting technology but using it mindfully to enhance our human experience rather than dictating it.

Will you join me on this journey of rediscovery and personal empowerment? By **Practicing the Pause,** we can balance the digital and the physical, reclaim our agency, and live a truly ours life. The choice is ours to make.

Lesson: This is how we Do It! Show Up!

***

Please make a Commitment to Show Up. It's the surest path to success. I've been in the personal and leadership development business for over 30 years, and the idea of "showing up" has never stopped. Agree to Show Up!

✓ You must first show up.

✓ Agree.

✓ Take Action.

✓ Practice Daily. Thirty days to make a habit.

✓ Showing up is the key to success.

2

Free Your Brain

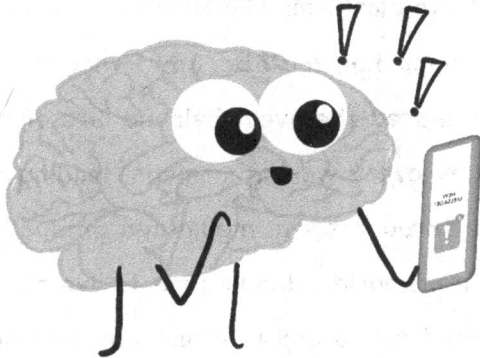

Unplug

I am a Computer Scientist and an Artist with a knack for getting to the detail, vision, and strategy, and I've seen firsthand how artificial intelligence has taken over our lives. It was like I had outsourced my experiences to algorithms and data points. In the past, I experienced the overwhelming trap of constant connectivity to platforms like Facebook, LinkedIn, Instagram, Snapchat, YouTube, and Twitter, where In the past, I shared the overwhelming lure of it which consumed my every waking moment., leading me to live my life through social media and gradually erasing my real-life memories., leading me to live my life through social media and progressively erasing my real-life memories.

One day, I realized I had lost touch with the world around me. I couldn't remember the last time I had a meaningful conversation with a friend or truly enjoyed a beautiful sunset. I decided then and there that I needed to take matters into my own hands and reclaim my life.

I stared at the world around me, so familiar yet so unfamiliar. Oh, how we, as followers of our defined Spiritual Being, are much like Dorothy's three compadres! Like the Lion, we yearn for courage. Like the Scarecrow, we thirst for wisdom. And like the Tin Man, we long for a heart.

With a mighty roar, the Lion believed he lacked the essence of bravery, facing countless battles, conquering his fears, and standing up for what was right. But little did he know that courage flowed through his veins, waiting to awake. He just needed someone to speak those truths into his soul, to reveal the roaring strength that lay dormant within him all along.

The Scarecrow, with his burlap mind, believed he lacked intelligence. He yearned for knowledge and understanding, unaware that his thoughts were teeming with brilliance. He had solved riddles, devised plans, and navigated through challenging situations

9

with surprising wit. He just needed someone to remind him of his innate wisdom, to untangle the threads of doubt and unravel the limitless potential of his mind.

And then there was the Tin Man, with his hollow chest. He felt empty, as if devoid of any capacity to love. Yet, he had shown compassion, empathy, and kindness countless times. He had comforted the broken-hearted, lent a helping hand to those in need, and shed tears for the pain of others. He just needed someone to point out that his heart beat with an unyielding love to reveal the warmth within him.

Dorothy, with an innocent gaze, saw through the facade of her three friends, knowing they possessed what they sought; they just needed it revealed. She became the voice they needed, the remainder of their inherent worth and potential. And as they journeyed through the perils of Oz, she unveiled the truths they had longed to hear.

Ultimately, they learned that the answers they sought might have been inside themselves. They were already courageous, wise, and compassionate. They needed someone to speak the truth and remind them of their qualities.

As I reflect on this journey to Unplug, I realize that we, too, are on a similar path. We have what we seek; we need it revealed. We have courage, wisdom, and love deep within us. We are more than we believe, capable of greatness beyond our imagination. And sometimes, all we need is a voice—a gentle reminder that the answers we seek are already within us.

Lesson: Commit to Unplug for Success
***

What does committing to Practicing the Pause Mean? Now! I've worked in leadership and personal development for over three decades, and in that time, I've seen the significance of committing remain unchanged.

✓ Put it on the calendar each day for 30 days.

✓ Say you will do it. **Practice the Pause.**

✓ Unplug from your devices.

✓ Take a 15-minutes.

✓ Write down the experience.

✓ And start again.

3

Do Not Disturb

* * *

90-20 Method

I woke up one morning and realized that my phone had become an inseparable part of my life. From the moment I opened my eyes, I would reach for it, and it would accompany me throughout the day.

The thought of breaking free from this addiction intrigued me.

So, I went to the park. As I sat in the garden, engrossed in my phone, I overheard two strangers discussing the detrimental effects of excessive phone usage.

I paid attention as they talked about the science behind smartphone addiction and gave practical tips on how to stop it.

Inspired by their conversation, I decided it was time to take control of my life and break free from the chains of phone addiction.

I began implementing the mentioned strategies, determined to reclaim my time and attention.

✓ First, I deactivated my accounts on platforms such as Facebook, LinkedIn, Instagram, Snapchat, YouTube, and Twitter;

✓ Second, I stopped my cell services, disconnecting from mobile networks and potentially limiting the functionality of my phone;

✓ Third, I took a break for 12 months, consciously choosing to abstain from social media and cellphone usage, granting myself a respite from constant connectivity; and

✓ Finally, I refocused my attention during this break, optimal productivity. ("52-17 method" or the "Pomodoro Technique") I walked away from my computer for around 20-30 minutes every 90 minutes I worked and redirected my attention towards myself and personal relationships, hobbies, self-reflection, and productivity while distancing myself from social media and cellphone distractions.

It is extreme, and taking charge of the phone's notifications or the relationship with the Social Media apps might make sense. So I tried a more straightforward approach; here's what I tried after 12 months.

A simple act of taking charge of the phone's notifications by disabling unnecessary alerts, putting the phone on "Do Not Disturb" mode to minimize distractions, and uninstalling addictive apps like Instagram and Facebook, opting to access them through a browser instead might be the ticket.

To establish a healthier relationship with my phone, I adopted the 90-20 Method.

Modifying "the 52-17 method" or the "Pomodoro Technique;" a time management method developed by Francesco Cirillo in the late 1980s, breaking your work time into intervals of 25 minutes, known as "pomodoros," followed by a short break of 5 minutes. After completing four pomodoros, you can take a more extended leave of 15-30 minutes.

In my case, I worked for 90 minutes and then took a break of 20 minute, 90-20 method. I was repeating this cycle throughout the workday. While it deviates slightly from the traditional 25-5 pattern, taking regular intervals to maintain focus and productivity remains the same.

By stepping away from my computer and engaging in activities unrelated to work, such as personal relationships, hobbies, self-reflection, or other productive tasks, I give myself time to recharge and refocus my attention. This approach helps prevent burnout, increase productivity, and reduce distractions from social media and cell phones.

It's important to note that while the 52-17 method has proven effective for many people, different individuals have different work styles and preferences. Feel free to adapt the technique to suit your needs and find the best balance.

Realizing that I often mindlessly checked my phone during short breaks, I challenged myself. I limited preventing my messages to three times daily, responding to them efficiently with voice notes. I designated two sessions daily for recreational apps like games and videos and checked my group chats only once daily. Instead of reaching for my phone, I engaged in activities that nurtured my well-being, such as meditation, stretching, or even taking short power naps, which helped me stay focused and avoid constantly checking my phone.

Regulating my time spent on social media became a priority. I set daily reminders on my apps to gradually reduce my usage. Starting with one hour, I gradually decreased it to 45 minutes, then 30 minutes, and so on. To hold myself accountable, I publicly displayed my target time and daily usage on a visible sheet of paper.

One of the most challenging habits to break was keeping my phone away from me at night. However, I understood the importance of disconnecting before bed, so I consciously tried to place my phone in another room. But I recognized that out of sight meant out of mind. I kept my phone far away in another room or locked in a cupboard. By making it less accessible, I was less likely to reach for it and fall back into old habits mindlessly. I also challenged myself to complete five small tasks in the morning before looking at my phone, allowing me to start the day with a clear focus.

I noticed a gradual shift in my behavior and mindset as I implemented these strategies. I have become more present now, more engaged with the world, and more in control of my time and attention. Breaking free from phone addiction wasn't easy, but the freedom it brought was worth every effort.

I can do it now, for a short time each day. I no longer need to look at my phone constantly. Instead, I observe nature's beauty, start conversations with strangers, and enjoy life's simple pleasures. Sitting in the park, I could feel the break in the chains of addiction and could see a healthier, more balanced lifestyle down the road.

Lesson: Silence the Noise

***

Breaking phone addiction requires effort and perseverance, but the benefits of regaining control over your time and attention are worth it.

✓ Use the 90-20 Method.

✓ Limit personal message checking 3x or less.

✓ Use recreational apps only twice a day.

✓ Check group chats only once a day.

✓ Phone as a task completion reward.

4

Practice the Pause

* * *

The Power of Practicing the Pause

I started by learning to **Practice the Pause**. It began with something as simple as turning off my notifications. Those constant pings and alerts had been dictating my life, pulling me away from the present moment. I created space for myself to breathe and think by silencing those distractions.

Practice the Pause refers to deliberately disconnecting from technology, specifically phones, devices, computers, and other digital distractions. It involves turning off or putting aside these devices, removing notifications, deactivating social media accounts, and creating a space free from the constant influx of information and digital noise. Start small, practice, and add more time. By practicing the Pause, individuals aim to create a break from the overwhelming presence of technology in their lives. It allows for stillness, introspection, and reconnection with the present moment.

I started journaling and meditating, cultivating a sense of mindfulness and self-awareness. I discovered that I didn't need to constantly consume information or seek validation from social media to feel fulfilled. Instead, I found fulfillment in moments of stillness and reflection. Practicing the pause allowed me to regain control over my thoughts and emotions.

During my year-long Practicing the Pause, my creative juices started flowing, and I began creating art by taking my paint brushes to canvas. Using my brush and the force of my imagination, I experienced the powerful satisfaction of rediscovering joy, self-expression, and accessing a reservoir of emotions.

Not only did my world shift, but I also realized the broader impact of my journey. Cutting-off access to technology reaffirmed the transformative potential of art for self-discovery and personal growth.

By taking control of my life and consciously engaging with creativity, I became less susceptible to the influence of artificial intelligence. I started to feel alive again, regaining my autonomy and reshaping my relationship with myself and technology. This newfound freedom gave me the time and mental space to carefully consider my decisions and choose a path aligned with my values.

In a society increasingly dominated by

algorithms and data-driven decisions, practicing the pause is an act of rebellion. It's a reminder that we are more than just data points and users. We are complex, sentient beings capable of deep connections, creativity, and growth.

So, please take a moment, turn off your notifications, and Practice the Pause. Embrace the power of **Practicing the Pause** and watch as your world shifts before your eyes. It may start with just a few minutes a day, but in time, it will lead to a genuine life free from the grasp of artificial intelligence. Like an Ironman, you will gain new experiences, find support, and move closer to your goals.

Lesson: The Power of Practicing the Pause
***

Practicing the Pause is an act of rebellion against the dominance of algorithms and data-driven decisions, reminding us of our complexity as sentient beings capable of deep connections, creativity, and growth. By embracing the power of the Pause, you can experience a transformative shift in your world, leading to a simple life free from the grasp of artificial intelligence. A few minutes a day dedicated to the Pause can pave the way for new experiences, support, and progress toward your goals.

✓ The Power of THE PAUSE.

✓ Disconnect from technology.

✓ Cultivate mindfulness and self-awareness.

✓ Engage in creative activities.

✓ Take control and reshape your relationship.

5

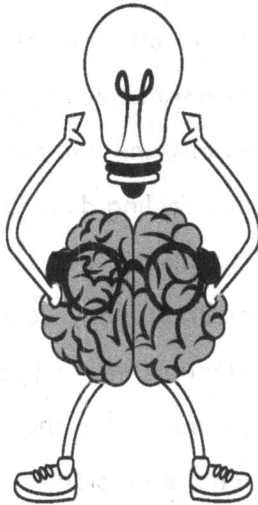

Take Action

* * *

Renew

The glow of the screens surrounded me as I sat in my cluttered workspace. Coding projects, emails, and social media notifications demanded my attention. But amidst the chaos, a wave of discontent washed over me. Something was off. I had become a slave to technology, and it was time for a change.

I closed my eyes and took a deep breath, allowing myself a moment of introspection. The realization hit me like a jolt of electricity. The allure of technology had overshadowed my true potential. The constant distractions and the never-ending stream of information left me feeling disconnected from myself and the world around me.

With determination in my heart, I embarked on a journey of disconnection, seeking solace from the constant digital noise and embracing the beauty and freedom that awaited me outside my window. I made a promise to myself, vowing not to let technology dictate my every move but to take control and

Practice the Pause, a mantra that would guide me on this transformative path.

With this mantra in mind, the silence that followed was both unnerving and liberating. For the first time in a long time, I felt tranquility. At that moment, I made a conscious choice to step into the comfort of the quiet stillness. It was time to reconnect with what truly mattered—to rediscover life's magic beyond the digital world's glow.

Taking more control of when I used technology reaffirmed the transformative potential for self-discovery and personal growth. And so, I continued my journey, each day, just for five minutes without it, embracing the beauty surrounding me, cherishing every encounter, and savoring the profound magic of rediscovery.

As the distracting pings, dings, and chaotic noise receded into silence, a world of exquisite beauty unfurled like a vibrant tapestry before my eyes. The chaos and distractions that once clouded my senses dissipated, revealing a realm of awe-inspiring wonders.

I stood in awe as nature's masterpiece unveiled itself in splendor. Sunlight cascaded through the emerald canopy of trees, painting a kaleidoscope of dancing shadows upon the ground. The delicate petals of flowers unfurled, releasing their sweet fragrances into the air, inviting me to immerse myself in their captivating beauty.

I strolled through parks, listening to the symphony of birdsong and feeling the gentle caress of the wind. I reconnected more with the people who mattered, diving into soul-stirring conversations that ignited my passion and reminded me of what mattered.

With a newfound determination to reclaim my life, I set forth on a path guided by the mantra Practice the Pause. It was a call to action, a reminder that I could shape my destiny and regain control over my time.

I created a dedicated space in my home—a sanctuary free from the constant buzzing and glowing screens. Here, I could retreat and immerse myself in the richness of the present moment.

I began by setting boundaries. I turned off notifications, silenced my phone, and closed unnecessary tabs on my computer. Whenever the urge to mindlessly scroll through social media or respond to every incoming email arose, I would remind myself of the importance of this journey.

Practicing the pause wasn't completely disconnecting from technology—it was about using it intentionally and mindfully. I recognized that technology could be a powerful tool, but I needed to regain control over how and when I engaged with it.

As I gradually disconnected, a sense of liberation washed over me. I reclaimed pockets of time that had previously slipped unnoticed, allowing me to focus on what truly mattered. The weight of constant digital obligations began to lift, and I felt a growing sense of freedom.

In the stillness I created, I rediscovered the joy of simple pleasures. I spent evenings engrossed in a captivating book, lost in the pages instead of the infinite scroll of social media feeds. I rekindled my love for art, embracing the beauty of painting and drawing without the distraction of notifications vying for my attention.

I opened myself up to a world of possibilities. I found solace in nature, venturing outside to immerse myself in its awe-inspiring beauty. The vibrant colors, the gentle rustling of leaves, and the crisp air scent became my sanctuary.

Embracing the pause allowed me to tap into my inner creativity. I started journaling, allowing my thoughts to flow freely onto the pages without the pressure of likes, comments, or judgments. This self-expression became a source of solace, clarity, and self-discovery.

With each passing day, the practice of pausing became more natural. I embraced the quiet moments, savoring them as a chance to recharge, reflect, and realign with my true desires and aspirations. I began to feel a sense of empowerment, as if I was regaining control over my time and, ultimately, my life.

I answered the call to action and was committed to reclaiming my time. As I continued my journey, little did I know that the true magic and transformation lay just beyond the horizon, waiting to unfold in the coming chapters.

Lesson: Mastering Stillness
***

Find fulfillment in the moments of stillness and inner reflection:

✓ By disconnecting.

✓ Setting boundaries.

✓ Embracing stillness.

✓ Exploring nature.

✓ Creating and Self-expression.

6

Stillness

* * *

Step in...

The mundane routine had transformed me outside the digital doppelgänger, and I was starting to see my true potential obscured beneath a shroud of virtual monotony. But little did I know that a grand adventure awaited me, igniting my spirit, unraveling my hidden powers, and launching me into a world of infinite possibilities! I started to see things in a whole new light.

I arrived at the address and honked the horn, echoing through the quiet neighborhood. After waiting a few minutes, I honked again, growing impatient. Old houses lined the street, their faded facades telling stories of years gone by. Since this would be the last ride of my shift, exhaustion tugged at my body, tempting me to drive away and call it a day. But something inside me urged me to stay, to see this through till the end.

Resigned, I parked the car and stepped out, footsteps echoing on the empty street. The air was still, and melancholy hung in the atmosphere. I walked up to the front door and knocked, the sound carrying a sense of urgency.

"Just a minute," came a frail, elderly voice from inside. I could hear shuffling and dragging across the floor. Time seemed to stretch, each passing moment filled with anticipation and a tinge of uncertainty.

After a long pause, the door creaked open, revealing a small woman in her 90s. She stood before me, fragile and delicate, like a porcelain doll from a bygone era. She wore a print dress that harkened back to when life was simpler and a pillbox hat adorned with a veil, reminiscent of somebody from a 1940s movie.

By her side, she clutched a small nylon suitcase, the weight of her life contained within it. As I looked past her, I noticed the apartment behind her. It was frozen as if no one had lived there for years. The furniture was shrouded in white sheets, like ghosts of forgotten memories. There were no clocks on the walls, no knickknacks or utensils on the counters. The emptiness was palpable, and the silence was deafening.

A cardboard box in the corner of the room sat, filled with faded photographs and delicate glassware. It felt like a time capsule, capturing the essence of a life that once thrived in this forgotten space.

"Would you carry my bag out to the car?" the woman asked, her voice filled with gratitude and vulnerability. I nodded, taking the suitcase in my hands, its weight a metaphor for her burdens. We walked slowly toward the waiting cab, her arm linked with mine.

She thanked me for my kindness, but I felt honored to be in her presence. "It's nothing," I assured her, my voice warmed. "I always treat people how I'd want them to treat my mom."

A faint smile tugged at her weathered lips, and her eyes sparkled with gratitude. "Oh, you're such a good boy," she whispered, and it felt like a gentle caress to my weary soul. We settled into the cab, and she provided an address, her request carrying a bittersweet weight.

"Could you drive through downtown?" she asked, her tone fragile and dreamy. "It's not the shortest way," I hesitantly replied. The practicality in me wanted to take the most direct route, but compassion guided my decision. "Oh, I don't mind," she said softly. "I'm in no hurry. I'm on my way to a hospice."

I glanced at her through the rear-view mirror, meeting her glistening eyes. It was as if the weight of her words hung heavy in the air, a reminder of life's fleeting nature. "I don't have any family left," she continued, barely above a whisper. "The doctor says I don't have very long." Her vulnerability touched a tender chord within me, and without hesitation, I reached over and shut off the meter.

"What route would you like me to take?" I asked, my voice gentle and understanding. In the silence that followed, we embarked on a journey through the city. She guided me, showing me the building where she had once worked as an elevator operator, her stories painting vivid pictures of a vibrant past. We drove through the neighborhood where she and her husband had shared their early years of love and companionship. She had me pull up in front of a furniture warehouse that had once been a ballroom where she had danced and twirled in the embrace of youth.

Sometimes, she would ask me to slow down in front of a particular building or a tight corner, and she would sit there, gazing into the darkness, lost in her thoughts. I respected her silence, understanding that memories were flooding her mind, weaving a tapestry of a life well-lived.

Her voice broke the stillness as the first hints of sunlight kissed the horizon. "I'm tired. Let's go now." She spoke with resignation and acceptance. We made our way to the address she had given me, the journey nearing its end.

It was a low building, a small convalescent home, its entrance framed by a portico. As soon as we pulled up, two orderlies emerged from the building; their gazes focused on her every move. They were expectant, prepared for her arrival.

I opened the trunk and carefully carried the small suitcase to the door. The woman was already seated in a wheelchair, her frail frame nestled within its embrace. A mixture of emotions filled the air - a sense of finality, of letting go, and a comforting presence of caretakers who would ensure her well-being.

"How much do I owe you?" she asked, her hand reaching into her purse, her voice tinged with gratitude and a sense of duty. "Nothing," I replied, a gentle smile on my lips. "You have to make a living," she responded, soft but insistent. I paused, meeting her gaze, and replied, "There are other passengers."

Almost instinctively, without analyzing the implications, I leaned forward and embraced her, holding her fragile form with tenderness and care. In that simple act of connection, she found solace and joy. "You gave an old woman a moment of joy," she whispered, her voice filled with appreciation. "Thank you."

I squeezed her hand gently, feeling the warmth of her touch. And then, with a heavy heart, I walked away, stepping into the dim morning light. Behind me, the door closed; it is sound, a profound echo, the closing of a chapter and the passing of a life.

The weight of that encounter lingered with me long after. Throughout the rest of that day, words failed me, for how could I convey the depth of what had transpired? The realization struck me with a forceful clarity. What if that woman had encountered an angry or impatient driver? What if I had refused to take the run, honked once, and driven away? The thought chilled me to the core.

On reflection, I realized that I had done something far more significant than any grand gesture I could imagine. In that fleeting encounter, I had been allowed to extend kindness and compassion, touch a life, and honor the dignity of a fellow human being.

We often deceive ourselves, led to believe that our lives revolve around monumental moments. Still, seemingly small acts of kindness can reshape lives and leave an indelible mark on the human spirit.

As the storyteller of this encounter, I share it with you, not with a request to forward it, but with the hope that it will resonate within you, igniting a spark of empathy and reminding you of the profound impact we can have on one another.

Life may not always be the grand party we envisioned, but we can see it if we open our eyes. And while we are here, we can dance, embracing the moments, big or small, that allow us to connect, care, and make a difference in the lives of others.

Lesson: Rebirth of a Hero.

One Year, Infinite Possibilities

***

Find a newfound calmness that lays the
foundation for the challenges and adventures ahead,
embracing the unknown with serenity and a steadfast
commitment to cherishing the present.

✓ Be a hero in the making.

✓ Form new companions that form true magic.

✓ Hold a brandished sword of determination.

✓ Push limits as trials test resolve.

✓ Triumph over challenges.

7

Sense

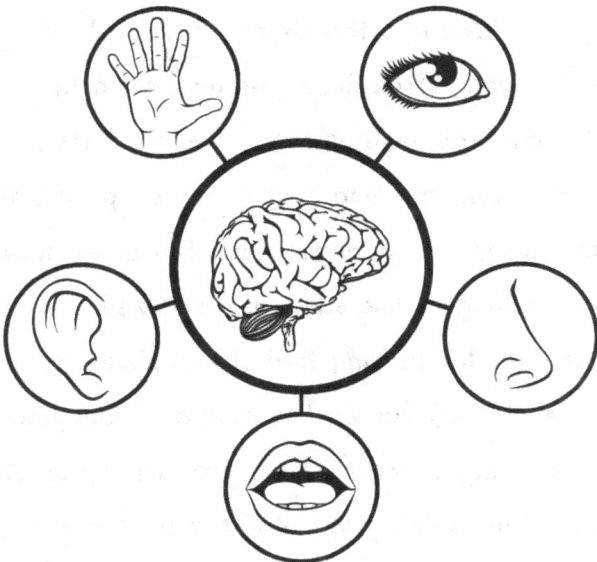

* * *

Awakening

I woke up that morning feeling a sense of restlessness. The sun was high, and the birds sang cheerful melodies outside my window. It was one of those in-between times, not a special occasion or a holiday, just an ordinary day with no particular plans or obligations. As I sat up in bed, I couldn't help but notice how time stretched before me, its moments lingering as if reluctant to move forward.

I shuffled into the kitchen, the smell of freshly brewed coffee filling the air. As I poured myself a cup, the minutes seemed to melt away. The steam rose from the mug, and I took a sip, savoring the rich flavor on my tongue. Time felt swift, slipping through my fingers like sand, as I realized I had lost track of it while enjoying that simple pleasure.

Leaving my cup on the counter, I stepped outside, basking in the sun's warmth. On my porch, I embraced the soothing touch of the sun's warmth while a gentle breeze brushed against my face. The air filled with a harmonious symphony of birdsong, whose intoxicating melodies resonated within me as the sweet perfume of budding flowers gracefully blended with the lively dance of the wind.

I am entirely present, allowing me to experience the unfolding of everything before me. The world around me was alive with activity, yet I felt a tinge of sadness lingering within. Time became a heavy weight upon my shoulders, each passing second a reminder of moments I wished could have lasted longer. The moments I let pass by because I wasn't aware. I heard the laughter of children playing nearby and the rustling of leaves in the gentle breeze —each sound carried a bittersweet beauty, mingling with the sadness within.

I made a cup of tea and enjoyed each sip, taking in all the flavors and smells. Being present with my senses gave me great satisfaction. I took long walks outdoors, connecting with the rhythm of my breath, and each stride became a meditation grounding me in the present moment. I relearned the joy of mental stimulation and movement.

Later, I found myself lost in a book, completely engrossed in its pages. The story transported me to another world, and hours slipped away unnoticed. The sensation of time became distorted, stretching and compressing as the narrative unfolded. It was as if the characters had taken hold of time, manipulating it to suit their whims.

The evening settled in, and I strolled through the nearby park. The setting sun painted the sky in hues of gold and pink, casting a warm glow over the world. Each step felt deliberate and purposeful as if I savored each passing moment. A feeling of curiosity led my hand to brush against the velvety petals of a rose. The softness and smoothness beneath my fingertips brought forth a tactile sensation that reminded me of the vast range of textures in the world. I explored further, running my hand over the rough bark of a tree, feeling the coolness of a smooth stone and the tickle of grass between my toes. Each touch awakened a sense of connection with the physical world, making me acutely aware of the diverse sensations experienced through touch.

The weariness of my thoughts receded into the background, replaced by a sense of tranquility. Time became a tranquil river, flowing gently, seemingly endless, as I immersed myself in the beauty of the world around me.

Night fell, and I returned home, feeling a sense of contentment. I curled up on the couch, my thoughts drifting to the people I held dear. Memories of loved ones, both near and far, filled my mind, and time seemed to crawl. Each cherished moment I played like a movie reel, capturing the joy, love, and laughter shared throughout the years.

As I drifted to sleep, I couldn't help but reflect on the profound truth of the saying, "Time is determined by feelings and physiological conditions and not by clocks." In the ordinary, in-between times of life, time morphed and danced to the rhythm of my emotions. It stretched, raced, twisted, and turned, all in response to the ever-changing landscape of my heart.

And so, I surrendered to the ebb and flow of time, knowing that its nature was as fickle as my own. With that understanding, I embraced the beauty and uncertainty of each passing moment, ready to embrace the stories that unfolded within the quiet spaces between life's grand celebrations. Then, I delved deeper into my practice of the pause, and a remarkable transformation grew within me. Stepping into stillness had opened the door to a world of heightened senses, where the ordinary became extraordinary, and every moment held a touch of magic.

I didn't realize that awakening the senses was just the start of my self-empowerment journey. The world was waiting, and I was eager to embrace it.

Lesson: Free from the AI Matrix!
***

Awaken special moments and empower yourself by living the special moments in-between.

✓ Restless morning.

✓ Fleeting moments

✓ FCherished connections.

✓ Surrendering to time's rhythm.

✓ Transformation through stillness.

8

Allies

* * *

Connect in Person

As I continued practicing the pause, I realized that the path to reclaiming my time was not one I had to tread alone. Along the way, I encountered like-minded individuals who had also recognized the need to step away from the constant distractions of the digital world. These encounters became the building blocks of powerful alliances, profoundly shaping my journey.

I made a serendipitous encounter with an old friend made me smile, and suddenly, time felt fleeting once more. We reminisced about shared memories and laughed at the silly anecdotes we'd collected over the years. The minutes flew by, leaving us craving for more time together. Taking a pause meant connecting with people. I paid attention to how people spoke, how their voices changed, and how their bodies showed how they felt. I was fully present in my relationships, listening and understanding without notifications.

Through local meetups and online communities,

I connected with fellow seekers of balance and authenticity. We shared stories, exchanged tips, and supported one another on our quest for a more mindful existence. I found solace and understanding in these spaces, knowing I was not alone in my desire to reclaim time and prioritize the present moment.

These newfound allies became more than just companions on the journey; they became pillars of strength and inspiration. We gathered in cozy cafes and serene parks, engaging in heartfelt conversations that flowed effortlessly without the interruptions of notifications. We laughed, we listened, and we indeed saw one another.

Together, we discovered the power of collective intention. We encouraged each other to stay committed to Practicing the Pause, offering gentle reminders in moments of temptation or doubt. We celebrated our victories, no matter how small, and lifted each other during times of challenge. In this web of support, we found the courage to face the unknown and embrace our true potential.

In addition to the human connections, I also encountered wise mentors. These individuals had traversed the path of self-discovery and had profound insights to share. They guided me with their wisdom and offered practical tools to navigate the complexities of life in a digital age.

These mentors ignited the fire, inspiring me to push past my limits and embrace my unique potential. Under their guidance, I deepened my understanding of the pause practice. I learned to cultivate mindfulness in every aspect of my life, not just during designated moments of stillness. I discovered the art of setting intentional boundaries with technology and reclaiming control over my attention and time.

As I forged connections with allies and mentors, I realized I was part of a more significant movement—a collective shift in consciousness. Together, we were rewriting the narrative of our relationship with technology. We were reclaiming our lives and rediscovering the beauty of the present moment.

The alliances I formed and the wisdom

imparted to me were invaluable. They gave me the strength to face the challenges that inevitably arose on this path of self-empowerment. They reminded me that I was not alone and were all in this together, united by a shared vision of a more balanced and fulfilling life.

In finding my allies, I discovered the immense power of community. Through the support and encouragement of these like-minded souls, I could tap into my inner strength and persevere. They became my tribe, my companions on this transformative journey of practicing the pause.

Little did I know that the friendships created in these times would transcend the journey and become lifetime connections that would inspire and encourage me long after I emerged from self-discovery. I was ready to face whatever obstacles lay ahead because I knew we were unstoppable with my allies on my side.

Lesson: Unplug, Awaken, and Ignite
***

Through connections with friends, mentors, and a larger community, we supported each other in staying committed to the practice and celebrating our victories. These relationships became pillars of strength, inspiring us to push past limits and embrace our true potential. Together, be a part of a collective shift in consciousness, rewriting the narrative of our relationship with technology.

✓ Path of pause, allies arise.

✓ Serendipitous smiles, mindful connections.

✓ Collective shift, rewriting the narrative.

✓ Stronger together, facing obstacles.

✓ Lifetime connections, unstoppable alliance.

9

Triumph

* * *

That Magical Moment

We tried it in tandem, and it worked. Could we take the easy test: "Can you turn off your device for fifteen minutes daily?"

While I was doing it, things started to pop. When it hit me, I felt like I'd hit the jackpot. How come I'm so happy? I was finally talking to my kid again—my long-lost friend. Then we walked. We chatted while sitting outdoors in lawn chairs. In the living room, we read. We shared it. We enjoyed every minute of unrestrained play in the open air.

We met on the patio to enjoy the sun's warmth. My daughter and I then sat in our chairs, facing one other with shared anticipation—a moment engraved in my memory. We had a heartfelt talk about many things, both small and big.

And suddenly, in a beautiful second, we hugged each other tight. A hug so long it appeared to go on forever, so full of emotion that no amount of words could ever do it justice. With that single action, we talked about how close we are and how much we love each other. Our souls were changed permanently by the warmth and comfort of that embrace that engulfed us.

I couldn't help but spread my arms widely and lose myself in the unadulterated delight of the moment because it was such pure bliss.

Something magical happened.

That beautiful moment seemed like finding a buried treasure—a timeless human experience. It became painfully evident how important and powerful genuine connection is. It served as a reminder that, despite all the chaos and diversions in life, the real richness is in our bonds with those we love.

We planned to play, go on road trips, and weekend mom-daughter time. We had fun talking in the great outdoors. We laughed as we walked.

I woke up! She woke up!

It happened this morning, yet I still feel it. I was talking to my child. She wasn't texting or sending a direct message, but rather, she was fully present.

However, I was also happy in other ways. The real highlight was spending quality time with my daughter.

And as I kept trying to unplug, each day, just fifteen minutes, I had more time to spend with my husband, mom, dad, and friends.

As we discussed each other's lives, the conversation flowed easily and covered various issues, from the everyday to the profound.

I relished hearing what they had to say without anything drawing me away. Being there with them was a deep experience, listening to their stories and learning from them.

As the practice day came to an end, I could feel it. I kept at it every day for a week. And as the week went on, our time together got much more. I recognized how precious what I had discovered was. It wasn't just a happy reunion or a casual chat; it was a confirmation of the enormous influence that human connection has on our lives. The experience taught me to value these times and true relationships that offer joy. I realized that life's greatest riches are love and connectedness with those we care about.

Lesson: Pause
***

Waking up brings magic: being present, cherishing loved ones, lasting happiness.

✓ Disconnecting from devices.

✓ It's powerful to agree to unplug for 15 minutes every day.

✓ There is power in genuine connection.

✓ Cherish relationships.

✓ Rediscover genuine connection:

10

Reborn Hero

Feel It

I was sitting among a large group of executives, and it was finally my turn to address the gathering. As I stood up, I felt a rush of anxiety. All eyes were on me, filled with curiosity and uncertainty. It had taken me hours of planning, organizing, and building trust in myself to reach this point. But I was determined to lead the movement toward freeing ourselves from excessive AI reliance, and I chose to lead by example in a public setting.

I felt a rush of anxious energy and butterflies of exhilaration.

I took a deep breath before moving forward, my voice resonating with conviction. The group consisted of people like me, diverse in experience and background, and I told them about my problems with being addicted to technology, how empty I felt, and how I realized that we were giving up real human connections for the draw of the digital world. In my talk, I discussed numerous studies and research showing AI's detrimental effects on human well-being and relationships. I stressed the need to reclaim control and repair technology-weakened ties.

I described how I used the Pause to create a healthier balance in my household by implementing phone-free zones, durations, or even days. I set limits with my family and friends, monitored use, and kept it to a minimum. Additionally, I set priorities and plans and had genuine face-to-face contact. I made a game out of it with penalties for breaking the rules.

I talked about what I did with my leisure time during my year-long practice, the Pause, eliminating technology by unplugging it, turning everything off, and closing things down. I provided fitness and health coaching to others. Some of my more measurable achievements were: running a half marathon in each of the 50 states; competing in an Ironman; traveling to other nations; taking road vacations with my daughter; becoming a writer and publishing books; and speaking at events worldwide.

I also learned a lot from it, including new experiences, inquiry, confronting risks, trying different things, reflecting on oneself, growth as an individual, collective shift, beating obstacles, forming lifelong friendships, establishing boundaries, enjoying outdoor adventures, taking part in creative activities, and working in mindfulness.

Their softened faces showed a common understanding, and their expressions lightened.

From that day forward, the movement gained momentum. People from all walks of life joined our cause—students, parents, professionals, and retirees. We organized workshops, seminars, and support groups, providing resources and strategies to help individuals break free from the grips of excessive AI. We promoted digital detoxes and encouraged people to designate screen-free zones in their homes and workplaces.

Over time our movement gained recognition, and governments and institutions noticed. They began implementing policies and guidelines to address the issue of excessive AI. Schools incorporated digital literacy programs, teaching young minds to navigate the digital world responsibly. Workplaces instituted technology boundaries, encouraging employees to disconnect during non-working hours. Slowly but surely, the tide began to turn.

Our journey had been challenging, but the rewards were immeasurable. I broke the chains of excessive AI, and we had woven a tapestry of human connection in their place. We had rediscovered the true essence of being human—to be present, connected, and free from the confines of a virtual world.

And as the sun set, casting its golden hues upon the horizon, I smiled, knowing that our forged bonds would endure, reminding us constantly of our power to shape our destiny.

Lesson: Reclaiming Our Connection.
***

Remember, technology is a tool that can enhance our lives if used mindfully and purposefully. By consciously managing our relationship with technology, we can break free from its potential adverse effects and create a healthier life balance.

✓ Phone-free zones creates a healthy balance.

✓ Turn it into a game with consequences for breaking the rules.

✓ Communicate boundaries with others.

✓ Track and limit device usage.

✓ Prioritize meaningful interactions and connections.

11

Hero

Have an Open Mind

At the airport, I couldn't resist a deal that enticed me with five donuts priced at $5. It was an irresistible offer, as it practically equated to buying three donuts at a regular price. I casually placed my belongings down and engrossed myself in the morning newspaper.

As I immersed myself in the business section, I noticed a man sitting across from me. Our eyes met briefly, exchanging a small smile and nod before I returned to my reading. A soft rustling sound from the table diverted my attention as I focused on reading the newspaper. Glancing over, I found myself surprised to see the man dipping his hand into the bag of donuts.

Initially, I felt a twinge of confusion, but it quickly dissipated. Judging by the man's appearance, I assumed he was homeless and in need of sustenance more than I was. Besides, I still had four donuts remaining, more than I intended to consume. With this reasoning, I reached into the bag, grabbed a donut, and resumed my newspaper perusal.

Lost in the social pages, I was interrupted yet again by the familiar rustling sound. Turning my gaze towards the table, I discovered the man's hand deep within the donut bag, taking another bite. I felt a surge of frustration rising within me. Why was he continuing to help himself to my donuts? Yet, hesitating to confront him, I forcefully retrieved another donut, silently expressing annoyance.

Time passed, and the loudspeaker called for the next departure, prompting the man to gather his belongings. As he approached the end of the table, something unexpected occurred. In my peripheral vision, I observed him reaching into the bag one last time, retrieving the last donut. However, instead of indulging, he broke it in half and extended one portion toward me. Perplexed, I couldn't help but exclaim my incredulity.

Overwhelmed by the sheer astonishment, I

tentatively accepted half of the donut, disbelief etched across my face. The man nodded, acknowledging our shared unspoken connection before departing from the scene.

As I sat there, contemplating the absurdity of the encounter, an announcement echoed through the airport, signaling the boarding of my flight. Hastily, I gathered my belongings, slipping on my jacket, unaware of the bag of donuts hidden beneath it. Then, I realized the truth—I had unknowingly been consuming the man's donuts while he remained silent, never complaining. And to add to the irony, he had kindly offered me his last donut, breaking it in half to share.

The experience left an indelible mark on my heart and mind. It taught me a profound lesson about the importance of not judging others based on appearances and assumptions. The man, whom I had initially perceived as an intruder, turned out to be a soul medicine of his own. His silent act of generosity and understanding resonated deeply within me.

Inspired by this encounter, I resolved to become more attentive, compassionate, and appreciative of the individuals who touch my life in various ways. I sought opportunities to spread kindness, lending a helping hand whenever possible and striving to see beyond the surface to understand and connect with others truly.

Ultimately, that chance meeting at the airport served as a poignant reminder that soul medicine can manifest itself unexpectedly in the form of those who love, support, and believe in us, even in the face of our misjudgments.

Appearances can be deceiving, but you will never notice if you aren't aware and have your head on the ground.

Actual acts of kindness show up from unexpected sources.

Don't judge others based on their appearance or circumstances, as we may overlook the genuine goodness and compassion they possess.

It emphasizes the importance of empathy,

understanding, and being open-minded in our interactions. It encourages us to be grateful for the people who touch our lives and never to underestimate the power of a simple act of kindness.

Being preoccupied with our distractions and judgments can also lead to overlooking the reality of a situation. By being absorbed in reading the newspaper and making assumptions about the person sitting across us, we miss essential cues and need help understanding the events unfolding before us. The story's moral is to remain attentive, open-minded, and present in our interactions, avoiding hasty judgments that may hinder our ability to perceive the truth.

Lesson: A Safe-space for Healthy Debates
***

This story teaches us to be alert, open-minded, and sensitive in our dealings. We learn to avoid snap judgments and unexpected value generosity. By using mindfulness, open-mindedness, not judging, and gratitude, we can build understanding, compassion, and deeper relationships with the people we meet.

✓ Increase your awareness.

✓ Avoid judgments.

✓ Cultivate empathy.

✓ Appreciate unexpected kindness.

Be...

✓ Mindful.

✓ Open-minded.

✓ Set aside assumptions about others.

✓ Gratitude.

12

Free-Zone

Experience It

In dreams, I've experienced vivid scenarios that sometimes take a while to fade away upon waking. It's not a big deal most of the time, and I quickly move on with my day. However, there was this one time in 6th grade when a dream turned my world upside down.

In this dream, my best friend and I had a massive falling out over something that now escapes my memory entirely. But let me tell you, it felt so real and intense that I woke up with a lingering anger that I couldn't shake off.

As a kid, I was notorious for holding grudges and not being the most forgiving soul. So, I completely ignored my best friend for three weeks, fueling my anger and frustration with each passing day. It got to the point where she couldn't take it anymore and broke down crying right in front of our friends.

Of course, as I started recounting the events

to the teacher, a sudden realization hit me like a ton of bricks. It all seemed so bizarre and unreal. I fell silent, glancing over at my devastated friend, and realized the magnitude of my mistake. I had screwed up royally.

I was at a loss for words, not knowing how to undo the damage I had caused. All because of a dream that felt all too real at the time. It was a moment of pure embarrassment and regret, and I couldn't help but feel like the biggest fool in the world.

From that day forward, I learned a valuable lesson about the power of dreams and the importance of distinguishing them from reality. And most importantly, I discovered the necessity of forgiveness and the danger of holding onto grudges. It's safe to say that I will never let a dream dictate my actions in such a disastrous way ever again.

***

With a heavy heart, I woke up in a chair at the airport waiting to board my plane, shaking, having to get my barrings, and feeling lost and disconnected from myself. My mistakes weighed heavily on my shoulders, and self-doubt crept in. Setbacks, heartaches, and drama clouded my vision, leading me astray. Somewhere along the way, I had veered off course, succumbing to old habits and losing sight of the path I had set out on.

However, deep within me, a flicker of determination ignited—a glimmer of hope that whispered, "It's not too late to find your way again."

Luckily, a compassionate flight attendant working that day lived by the philosophy of seeking goodness in the world, walked toward me, crouched down, and smiled.

"You're in the airport," she said, "Don't worry; your flight won't board for another hour."

My heart slowed, and I felt at ease.

It was a bright summer day; as she took a flight to Washington, she witnessed a heartwarming act of kindness that would forever leave an impression on her.

A little 94-year-old lady caught my eye as she made her way through the crowded terminal and aboard the plane. She looked fragile and worn out as she searched for her seat. Her face had a hint of bewilderment, reflecting the unpredictability of her adventure. My desire to help the older woman grew as my heart grew empathic.

At that moment, hope entered my heart.

A gentleman seated nearby caught sight of the elderly lady's struggle and instantly got up, filled with warmth and compassion; he beckoned the flight attendant over, eager to contribute to this unfolding tale of kindness.

"Could you please assist her in taking my seat, and I will gladly occupy hers?" said the guy meekly. She thanked him, and they approached the fragile lady. The guy walked beside her, his genuine smile lighting up the aisle. He gave off a strong sense of goodwill.

He extended his arm when he reached the older woman, providing her comfort and reassurance.

Her eyes welled with tears of appreciation at this unexpected act of kindness, and a bright smile lit up her face. She hugged him firmly, an embrace of thanks and connection.

I appreciate it, young man. 'Never in my 94 years has someone shown me such care,' she said in a calm, choked voice. As word rippled across the airport gate, guests felt delight and warmth. The new altitudes lifted everyone's mood as people realized the significance of even the simplest gestures of kindness. Compassion and unity transformed the airport.

I stood transfixed, my eyes fixated on the unfolding spectacle of compassion. In that transformative moment, the extraordinary power of reaching out and displaying genuine empathy was bare before me. Like a pebble, the simple act of kindness dropped into a calm lake and sent ripples cascading through the airplane, touching the hearts of every soul on board.

In a world often besieged by chaos and unrest, this profound encounter served as a luminous beacon, illuminating the innate goodness within humanity's core. It was a gentle nudge, urging all fortunate enough to bear witness to seek grand and humble opportunities to uplift others and forge precious connections.

As the patrons boarded their flight, my heart soared in happiness.

Seated comfortably in her assigned spot, I settled into my seat, a serene contemplation filling her mind. The spectacle of the human connection she had witnessed lingered in her thoughts like a delicate wisp of a memory. As the airplane propelled forward, traversing the ethereal expanse of the sky, it felt like the air around her echoed that transformative encounter.

The stewardess, a figure of grace and warmth, moved about the cabin attending to the needs of the passengers. With each interaction, she displayed a genuine concern for the well-being of those in her care, infusing the journey with palpable compassion. There was a certain radiance about her, as if she, too, carried the profound lessons etched deeply within her heart.

In the tranquil ambiance of the cabin, she was finding solace and inspiration. The flight attendant symbolized the powerful impact one person can have when they are friendly and empathetic. One person with a heart full of love and generosity became a symbol of the incredible influence, reshaping the stewardess. And as the airplane soared toward its destination, she couldn't help but reflect on her purpose and role in fostering human connection and spreading the light of compassion.

In the bustling cabin, I contemplated the power within me, the ability to touch lives, uplift spirits, and forge connections. With each passing moment, my resolve grew more assertive. Vowing to embody the same spirit of care and genuine concern I had witnessed in the stewardess, and I finally understood that the smallest gestures of compassion could ignite a chain reaction of love and unity.

With renewed determination, I embraced my

role as a passenger, not only in the literal sense but as a participant in the shared journey of humanity. In the boundless expanse of the sky, I allowed the lessons etched within my heart to guide me, to infuse every interaction with kindness and understanding, for I knew that in this vast tapestry of existence, it is through such connections, both big and small, that the true beauty of life unfolds.

The kindness witnessed became a catalyst for personal transformation. With unwavering resolve, I promised to seek out seemingly insignificant moments where I could make a difference and sow seeds of kindness in a world hungry for its tender touch.

Renewed with hope, I embarked on my journey, armed with a profound belief that even the smallest gestures of compassion possessed the power to pierce through the darkest of nights. In a world yearning for goodness, I understood that by choosing to embody goodness myself, I, too, could ignite a magnificent chain reaction of benevolence that transcends the boundaries of time and place.

I got off that plane renewed, stepping out of the airport doors with a renewed sense of being.

Still, this moment, this fresh chapter in my life, offered the promise of a brighter tomorrow. As the sun painted the sky with hues of gold and amber, unwavering determination coursed through my veins, intertwining the past with trials and tribulations. With every step forward, I carried a renewed sense of purpose, as if the universe whispered its blessings upon my path.

Embracing the dawn of a new day, I stepped onto the threshold of this grand adventure with a heart brimming with optimism and grace. The world lay before me like a vast canvas, ready to be painted with the strokes of my dreams and aspirations. Each breath I took infused me with the intoxicating scent of possibilities as if the air whispered secrets of untold wonders waiting to discover.

In a world often besieged by chaos and unrest, this profound encounter served as a luminous beacon, illuminating the innate goodness within humanity's core. It was a gentle nudge, urging all fortunate enough to bear witness to seek grand and humble opportunities to uplift others and forge precious connections.

As the patrons boarded their flight, my heart soared in happiness.

Seated comfortably in her assigned spot, I settled into my seat, a serene contemplation filling her mind. The spectacle of the human connection she had witnessed lingered in her thoughts like a delicate wisp of a memory. As the airplane propelled forward, traversing the ethereal expanse of the sky, it felt like the air around her echoed that transformative encounter.

The stewardess, a figure of grace and warmth, moved about the cabin attending to the needs of the passengers. With each interaction, she displayed a genuine concern for the well-being of those in her care, infusing the journey with palpable compassion. There was a certain radiance about her, as if she, too, carried the profound lessons etched deeply within her heart.

In the tranquil ambiance of the cabin, she was finding solace and inspiration. The flight attendant symbolized the powerful impact one person can have when they are friendly and empathetic. One person with a heart full of love and generosity became a symbol of the incredible influence, reshaping the stewardess. And as the airplane soared toward its destination, she couldn't help but reflect on her purpose and role in fostering human connection and spreading the light of compassion.

In the bustling cabin, I contemplated the power within me, the ability to touch lives, uplift spirits, and forge connections. With each passing moment, my resolve grew more assertive. Vowing to embody the same spirit of care and genuine concern I had witnessed in the stewardess, and I finally understood that the smallest gestures of compassion could ignite a chain reaction of love and unity.

Lesson: Growth
***

Without a personal gadget, you get a lesson that collectively drives growth, positive connections, and a mindset of understanding, kindness, and tenacity in managing life's issues. You gain:

✓ Self-reflection.

✓ Resilience.

✓ Compassion.

✓ Human connection.

✓ Forgiveness.

13

Personal Growth

Empathy

Landing safely, I headed to the terminal. Then, I boarded the public bus with a sense of weariness, hoping for a smooth journey to my destination. As I stepped into the vehicle, I stood face-to-face with the bus driver. The lady before me made an unusual gesture without uttering a single word. She stuck her thumb on her nose and playfully waved her fingers at the driver. It was an odd sight, but the driver seemed to understand.

The driver, clearly engaged in this silent conversation, placed his left hand on his right bicep and jerked his right arm up in a defiant fist. To my surprise, the bus driver reciprocated the gesture, raising his hands and wiggling his fingers. Not to be outdone, the lady extended her right arm and swiftly chopped at it a few times with her left hand.

Curiosity mingled with confusion within me as I watched the peculiar exchange unfold. The lady's next move intensified the already bizarre situation. She cupped both hands under her breasts and lifted them gently as if making a suggestive gesture. Without hesitation, the driver mirrored her action, placing both hands at his crotch and mimicking the lift.

My bewilderment peaked at this point, unable to comprehend the meaning behind these gestures. And just when I thought things couldn't get any stranger, the lady frowned, ran a finger up between her derriere, and abruptly called off the bus. I was left utterly stunned, my eyes wide with disbelief.

As the lady departed, I noticed another woman seated in the front row who had witnessed the entire perplexing exchange. She couldn't contain her shock and disapproval, yelling out her outrage at the driver's behavior. "That was the most disgusting thing I have ever seen on a public bus! What the hell were you doing?"

Maintaining his composure despite the accusation, the bus driver responded gruffly, "Listen, lady, the woman who boarded the bus before you was a deaf-mute. She communicated with me through gestures. She asked if the bus went to 5th Street, and I informed her that we had gone to 10th Street. She inquired about the number of stops, and I assured her that this was the express route. When she asked about the dairy, I said we passed by the ballpark. In response, she exclaimed, 'Shit, I'm on the wrong bus!' and promptly disembarked."

The revelation shocked me, realizing I had witnessed not some lewd exchange but a misunderstood conversation between two individuals with unique communication methods. It served as a reminder that appearances can often deceive, and we should be cautious in passing judgment based on limited information.

As the bus continued, I couldn't help but reflect on the importance of understanding and empathy. We should all strive to be more patient and open-minded, considering there may be more to a situation than meets the eye.

I stood there, perplexed, watching the strange

exchange between the lady and the bus driver. The gestures they were making seemed vulgar and inappropriate, and I couldn't help but feel a sense of disgust. When the lady finally got off the bus, unable to contain my shock, I spoke up.

"That was the most disgusting thing I have ever seen on a public bus! What the hell were you doing?" I exclaimed, unable to hide my outrage. The words slipped out before I could think twice.

The bus driver turned to face me; his expression was unchanged despite my outburst. In a gruff voice, he explained, "Listen, lady, the woman who got on the bus before you was a deaf mute. She couldn't speak, so she used gestures to communicate with me."

I felt a pang of guilt and embarrassment as his words sank in. My initial judgment had been based solely on appearances, without considering the possibility of alternative means of communication. It was a harsh reminder that I should never judge a book by its cover.

The bus driver continued his explanation, recounting the questions people who are hard of hearing women had asked him. She had been seeking directions, inquiring about the bus route and the number of stops. The driver had responded with corresponding gestures, trying his best to understand her and provide the information she needed. It was a simple miscommunication, not the lewd exchange I had assumed.

I felt remorse wash over me as I realized my mistake. I had let snap judgments cloud my perception and jumped to conclusions without knowing the whole story. This experience taught me a valuable lesson about empathy and understanding.

I learned that appearances can be deceiving, and it's essential to approach situations with an open mind. We should strive to understand others, even if their methods of communication are different or unfamiliar to us. Empathy and compassion are vital in avoiding misunderstandings and promoting harmony.

From that day forward, I resolved to be more

patient and less quick to judge. I understood the importance of seeking clarity and gathering all the facts before passing judgment. This encounter served as a poignant reminder that we should never underestimate the power of empathy and the value of truly understanding others.

During the chaos, I found myself immersed in the messiness of life. The world around me seemed overwhelming, with its complexities and unpredictability. It was as if I had been thrown into a turbulent swimming pool, struggling to reach the surface for a breath of air.

I recognized that avoiding challenges and uncertainties would only lead to a stagnant existence. But instead of burying my head in a hole or hiding away, I confronted it head-on. I embraced the chaos and allowed myself to experience life in all its rawness.

Living in the thick of it, I learned to navigate the waves of chaos with resilience and adaptability. I encountered moments of joy, triumph, setbacks, and disappointments. But through it all, I embraced the unpredictability, knowing it was an integral part of the human experience. Each day became an opportunity for growth and self-discovery.

The lessons I learned from the bus incident were a constant reminder. I sought understanding and empathy in my interactions with others, recognizing that we are all on our journeys, grappling with our challenges. I approached each situation open-heartedly, willing to see beyond the surface.

In the chaos, I discovered hidden pockets of beauty and moments of clarity. It was amidst the whirlwind that I found strength and resilience within myself. I learned to trust my instincts and to rely on my inner compass when the external world seemed tumultuous.

If I were to be plugged in, unaware of what just happened, I would have missed this intimate, precious-beautiful experience and realized that life did not adhere to being neatly packaged or perfectly controlled. It was messy, unpredictable, and often challenging. But it was in embracing this messiness that I truly lived. In the depth of the chaos, I discovered my capacity for growth and transformation.

As the bus continued its journey, I held onto this newfound perspective. With each passing day, I dove deeper into the pool of life, embracing the unknown and finding solace during the chaos. The world's chaos no longer overwhelmed me; instead, it became a canvas on which I could paint my own story.

Lesson: Unlocks infinite possibilities
***

You could ask yourself, "So where are the steps, the framework, and the outcomes I can take with me?" We will keep shifting our viewpoints, pay attention to the inner guide, and welcome the "softer" trip—one untidy or uncertain but wise and clear—in the quiet place that the moment of Pause creates. By using what you've learned and the tools given to you, you'll be better able to deal with life's challenges. You'll also have gained wisdom, compassion, courage, and faith. Hold their attention.

    ✓ Tools/Resources.

    ✓ Positive mindset.

    ✓ Clear goals.

    ✓ Supportive network.

    ✓ Self-confidence.

14

Powerful

* * *

And... Live Healthier Ever After

Looking back on my journey, filled with a profound sense of fulfillment and gratitude. Practicing the Pause has not only transformed my life but has also ignited a ripple effect, inspiring countless individuals to embark on their path of self-empowerment.

In the wake of my story and the collective efforts of a growing movement, the world has undergone a remarkable shift. The once all-consuming grip of technology has loosened its hold, replaced by a collective yearning for a more balanced, intentional existence.

Through public speaking engagements, workshops, and digital platforms, I continue to share my experiences and insights, inspiring others to reclaim their time, embrace the power of the Pause, and embark on their transformative journeys. The stories of individuals who have heeded the call resonate deeply, reaffirming the impact of practicing mindfulness and intentional living.

Communities have flourished, creating spaces for meaningful connections, creativity, and self-reflection. Digital wellness has become an integral part of education systems, nurturing the minds of the younger generation and equipping them with the tools to navigate the digital landscape with wisdom and discernment.

Workplaces have transformed, fostering a culture of balance and well-being. Employers recognize that productivity and innovation arise from a workforce not overwhelmed by constant distractions but nurtured through Practicing the Pause and reflection moments.

Families have rediscovered the joy of being fully present with one another. Screens no longer dominate meal times or gatherings but serve as tools for connection and inspiration when used intentionally and mindfully. Technology has become a servant rather than a master, amplifying the human experience rather than overshadowing it.

In this epilogue, I stand as a witness to the collective awakening that has taken place. The world is full of harmony, authenticity, and purpose. Practicing the Pause has become a guiding principle, shaping every aspect of our lives and reminding us of the beauty and infinite possibilities in the present moment.

But this story is not mine alone. It is the culmination of the efforts of countless individuals who have embraced their own hero's journey. Together, we have reshaped the world, honoring the essence of being human in a technologically-driven era.

As the curtain falls on this chapter of my life, I step forward, knowing that the legacy of Practicing the Pause will endure. I am filled with hope, knowing that the power to transform lies within each of us. By embracing the Pause, we can reclaim our time, awaken our senses, triumph over challenges, and inspire others to embark on their journey of self-empowerment.

The epilogue of my story is not an end but

rather a beginning—a call to action for all who yearn for a more balanced, mindful, and purposeful existence. Together, let us continue to inspire, uplift, and create a world where the Power of Practicing the Pause unlocks our true potential, reshapes our reality, and brings forth a future filled with presence, connection, and infinite possibilities.

Lesson: Call to Action

***

Are you tired of constantly being glued to your devices, missing out on meaningful connections with your loved ones? It's time for a change. Let's start a movement encouraging us to break free from our screens and rediscover the joy of face-to-face interactions. Imagine the laughter; so, here's the challenge:

✓ put down your device,

✓ turn off those notifications, and

✓ step out into the world to meet with your family and friends.

Will you join this movement for more genuine connections and happier relationships? Let's create moments that matter. Act now, and together, let's make a real difference in our lives and those we care about.

About the Author

Kim Groshek is a multi-talented individual who wears many hats. Besides being an author, she is a loving mother, devoted wife, accomplished Ironman Athlete, skilled artist, visionary entrepreneur, experienced senior consultant, and a seasoned female entrepreneur with over three decades of corporate experience. She overcame her aversion to social media and technology by using tried-and-true methods to rebuild herself and help others do the same.

Find out more about Kim Groshek at https://www.amazon.com/author/kmgroshek Or visit our events practicing the pause https://pausepower.online

Foreword

Kim's determination and authenticity deeply inspired me. Our paths crossed during a running adventure, where I witnessed her remarkable achievement of completing a half marathon in her fiftieth state and crossing the finish line as an Ironman. We met again during her captivating TEDx keynote, where her relatable nature and likable personality left a lasting impression. Her story ignited personal growth and empowerment, sparking a transformative journey within me.

Join our growing community of individuals touched by Kim's inspiring journey. It's an opportunity to be influenced by someone genuinely remarkable. Prepare for a transformative journey of self-discovery and embrace the power of authenticity as Kim's story illuminates your path. Let her inspiration guide you towards a more fulfilling life.

Other Books BY Kim Groshek

https://www.amazon.com/author/kmgroshek

If you enjoyed this book, found it useful or otherwise then I'd really appreciate it if you would post a short review on Amazon. I do read all the reviews personally so that I can continually write what people are wanting. If you'd like to leave a review then please visit this link: https://www.amazon.com/author/kmgroshek

Thanks for your support!

Can I Ask a Favor?

I'm excited that you have read Practice the Pause!

I'm on a mission to help everyone change their relationship with technology. Would you help me spread this

Pause Power Challenge visit our events supporting each other as we Practiice the Pause

https://pausepower.online AND

Join us on on Facebook, https://www.facebook.com/groups/pausepowerchallenge/

and get your family and friends involved.

It's simple!

Pause for 15-minutes or more a day.

Even go further to create a program in your

community!

Let's support each other and make our human connection happen!

Spread the word by email and mouth to any family and friends?

Notes

    "Brainy" says that's it for now but wants to challenge you! Practice the Pause! Try it. Start just fifteen minutes a day, then gradually add more time away. When you find yourself trapped and caught up in your technology, make a consorted effort to put your things aside and walk away from your device.

    Let's do this together.

    LIFE HAPPENS

    PAUSE HELPS!

Back Cover

***

Take a Pause.

TAKE A BREAK!

www.ingramcontent.com/pod-product-compliance
Lightning Source LLC
Chambersburg PA
CBHW011034050426
42335CB00055B/2863